Quilting Worksnops

Compiled by the editors of *Traditional Quiltworks* magazine

Techniques & Patterns from:
Jean Wells
Diana McClun & Laura Nownes
Mary Ellen Hopkins
Bettina Havig
Patricia Campbell
Nancy Brenan Daniel
Beverly Dunivent
Jan Krentz

CHITRA PUBLICATIONS
Your Best Value in Quilting

First Printing: 2000
Library of Congress Cataloging-in-Publication Data

Quilting workshops : techniques & patterns from Jean Wells, Diana McClun & Laura Nownes, Mary Ellen Hopkins, Bettina Havig, Patricia Campbell, Nancy Brenan Daniel, Beverly Dunivent, Jan Krentz / compiled by the editors of Traditional quiltworks magazine.
    p.cm.
    ISBN 1-885588-32-1
    1. Quilting—Patterns. 2. Patchwork—Patterns. I. Traditional quiltworks.
    TT835 .Q5475 2000
    746.46—dc21   00-021576

Edited by: Nancy Roberts
Design and Illustrations: Brenda Pytlik
Cover Photography: Guy Cali Associates, Inc., Clarks Summit, Pennsylvania
Inside Photography: Van Zandbergen Photography, Brackney, Pennsylvania, unless otherwise noted.
Thank you to all the teachers for kindly providing portrait photos.

Our Mission Statement:
We publish quality quilting magazines and books that recognize, promote and inspire self-expression. We are dedicated to serving our customers with respect, kindness and efficiency.

Are you like many busy quilters with limited time for taking a quilting class? Or do you simply prefer to learn at your own pace at home? Whichever situation applies to you, this book is sure to help. It's a collection of popular "Private Workshop" features from *Traditional Quiltworks* magazine. Each lesson is presented by a widely recognized quilting professional so you're sure to learn as you sew.

These projects span the seasons and include a special Christmas quilt. They also range in size from a single appliqué block you can use to make a pillow to full-size quilts that will grace any bed. The variety of construction methods introduced in the projects will help you develop the well-rounded skills every quilter desires. For example, master perfect points and round circles when you follow Pat Campbell's needleturn appliqué instructions. Or try your hand at stenciling a lovely holiday quilt with Nancy Brenan Daniel. Freezer paper stencils make it simple to do. Use fabric scraps for a time-honored method known as string piecing. Beverly Dunivent tells you how.

You'll also learn time-saving techniques to use in these projects and other projects you make. Mary Ellen Hopkins teaches how to make streamlined Rail Fence blocks and shows how to use them to make a lively and colorful quilt. Bettina Havig shares a no-template Amish-style wallhanging made with chain-pieced triangles. Jan Krentz offers a delightful hearts-and-houses wall quilt that includes foundation piecing and Danish Heart blocks with an interesting interwoven look.

Favorites such as House and Log Cabin blocks get an up-to-the-minute look. The "Madison House" pattern is from Diana McClun and Laura Nownes. Jean Wells' "Autumn Pines" contains Log Cabin and Tree blocks. Both patterns rely on no-template construction methods.

Page through the book and savor the big, full-color photos. Inspiration is sure to strike and you'll be ready to begin your private quilting lessons after just one look. The only travel involved is a short walk into your sewing room or a fun trip to your local quilt shop for just the right fabrics. Ready—set—sew!

The editors of
Traditional Quiltworks

The editorial team, clockwise from the top, Jack Braunstein, Debra Feece, Deborah Hearn, Elsie Campbell and Joyce Libal.

Contents
Projects and Biographies

Sparkling Star

Half-square triangles make the "sparkle" in this Amish-inspired scrap quilt!

A quiltmaker for nearly three decades and a former quilt shop owner, Bettina Havig has earned a long list of credentials in quilting. She's a teacher, author, quilt appraiser, judge, quilt historian and consultant. She has traveled throughout the United States, England and Europe to present classes and judge quilt shows. Her interest in historic quilts is evidenced by her serving as director of the Missouri Heritage Quilt Project, an effort to record 19th-century quilts in her home state. Bettina is president of the Quilt Conservancy, a non-profit organization that assists museums in acquiring vintage quilts. Her research led to publication of her latest book, *Carrie Hall Blocks* (AQS, 1999). This reference book documents more than 800 of author Carrie Hall's pieced and appliquéd blocks from a museum collection. Bettina provides pattern pieces and assembly diagrams for many of them. As a consultant for Silver Dollar City in Branson, Missouri, Bettina developed the concept for the annual quilt challenge and curated the traveling exhibit of participants. In addition to numerous articles in quilting magazines and her most recent book, Bettina has authored several books, including *Missouri Heritage Quilts* (AQS), *Amish Quiltmaker* (Sterling Publishers), *Quilts of the Booneslick Trail Quilters' Guild* (ASN) and *Amish Kinder Komforts* (AQS). Bettina favors hand piecing and hand quilting for her traditional quilts. The "Sparkling Star" quilt she shares here is an example of one of her Amish-inspired quilts.

Contact information:
Bettina Havig, 1108 Sunset Lane,
Columbia, MO 65203-2253

After curating a display of Amish crib and doll quilts from the collection of Sarah Miller for the Museum of the American Quilter's Society, I wrote patterns for some of the quilts. They were published in *Amish Kinder Komforts* (AQS, 1996). However, I like to remind quilters that only the Amish can make Amish quilts; the rest of us make Amish-style quilts. Choose bright solid fabrics for your version of this Amish-style "Sparkling Star."

QUILT SIZE: 34 3/4" square
BLOCK SIZE: 13 1/2" square

MATERIALS
Yardage is estimated for 44" fabric.
• 1 yard dark background such as black, navy, burgundy, forest green, eggplant, or dark charcoal
• Scraps or fat quarters (11" x 22") of at least 20 different solid colors
NOTE: *You may include different shades and tints of the same hue.*
• 3/8 yard fabric for the binding
• 1 1/8 yards backing fabric
• 38" square of low-loft batting

CUTTING
Dimensions include a 1/4" seam allowance.
• Cut 24: 2" x 22" strips, assorted solid colors, then cut ten 2" squares from each strip. Cut the squares in half diagonally, to yield 480 right triangles, you will use 472.
• Cut 16: 3 7/8" squares, background fabric
• Cut 24: 4 1/4" squares, background fabric, then cut them in half diagonally to yield 48 triangles
• Cut 4: 2 3/4" x 14" strips, background fabric, for the sashing
• Cut 4: 2 3/4" x 29 3/4" strips, background fabric, for the borders

NOTE: *You may wish to cut sashing and border strips a little longer to allow for possible variations in the 1/4" seam allowance.*
• Cut 4: 2 1/2" x 44" strips, for the binding

PIECING
• Chain piece pairs of right triangles, right sides together, to make 164 small pieced squares. You'll use 144 for the stars and 20 for the pinwheels in the sashing and border.
• Lay out 3 small pieced squares and 3 right triangles as shown. Stitch them into rows, then join the rows to make a pieced triangle. Make 48. Try to abandon your inhibitions about what "matches" and let the fabric work some magic in these units.
• Lay out 12 pieced triangles with 12 background fabric triangles and four 3 7/8" background fabric squares, as shown. Join

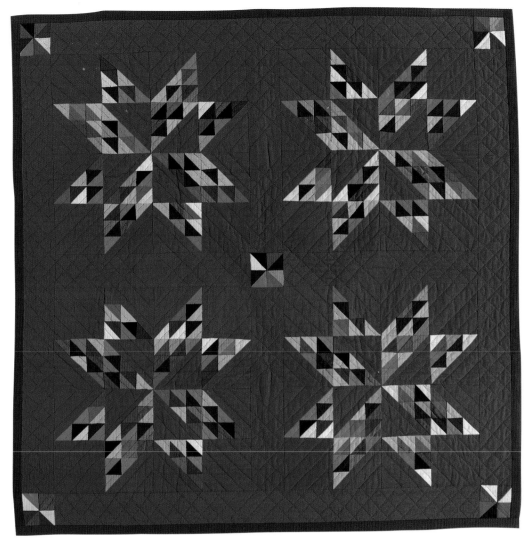

*Over 20 different solid colors went into **"Sparkling Star"** (34 3/4" square) by Bettina Havig of Columbia, Missouri. Bettina says, "forget about what matches and just let the fabric work some magic for you" in this Amish-inspired scrap quilt.*

Assembly Diagram

the triangles in pairs to make large pieced squares. Stitch the pieced squares and background fabric squares into rows. Join the rows, matching seams, to complete a Sparkling Star block. Make 4.

• Use 4 small pieced squares to make a Pinwheel block by stitching pieced squares in pairs and then joining the pairs to complete the block, as shown. Make 5.

• Stitch a 2 3/4" x 14" background fabric strip between 2 Sparkling Star blocks to make a pieced row. Make 2.

• Sew a Pinwheel block between the remaining 2 3/4" x 14" background fabric strips to make a pieced sashing strip.

• Referring to the Assembly Diagram, stitch the pieced sashing strip between the 2 pieced rows to complete the quilt center.

• Sew 2 3/4" x 29 3/4" background fabric strips to opposite sides of the quilt center.

• Stitch Pinwheel blocks to both ends of each of the remaining 2 3/4" x 29 3/4" background fabric strips. Sew them to the remaining sides of the quilt center.

• Finish the quilt as described in the *General Directions*, using the 2 1/2" x 44" strips for the binding.

I suggest using an all-over geometric grid as a quilting design.

_____QW

Folkloric Christmas

Use freezer paper stencils for this unique painted quilt.

Nancy Brenan Daniel's unique quilts are a result of her interest in a wide range of quiltmaking techniques along with years of study in the arts. After earning college degrees in both fine arts and art history, Nancy spent many years in the classroom, teaching art in both public school and at the college level. She also taught quiltmaking and joined two partners in opening the Quilters' Ranch, a shop in Tempe, Arizona. Eventually, Nancy sold her share and moved on to become a freelance designer and artist working from her studio at home. Nancy's designs include award-winning garments, dolls and soft sculptures in addition to quilts. She is a National Quilting Association (NQA) certified teacher and quilt judge. Nancy offers basic and advanced classes for quilters and dollmakers. Her class titles include "Color Play," "The Three-Minute Feathered Wreath" and "Grandma's Quilting Stitch." The author of 15 needlework books since 1985, Nancy publishes her books through her own firm as well as through The American School of Needlework (ASN). Several of her recent titles include *Learn How to Hand Quilt in Just One Day* (ASN), *Learn to Do Appliqué in Just One Weekend* (ASN), *Log Cabin Flower Quilts* (ASN), *Fine Feathers for Hand Quilters* (Brenan Daniel Publications) and *Folkloric Designs* (Brenan Daniel Publications). The latter contains original designs suitable for stenciled quilts, one of Nancy's favorite techniques and the one she includes here in her "Folkloric Christmas" quilt.

Contact information:
Nancy Brenan Daniel, PO Box 27757,
Tempe, AZ 85285 • E-mail: QultFrFn@aol.com

Someone once asked why I enjoy making stenciled quilts. Hist examples of stenciled quilts have a spontaneity of design I find charm and full of life. I enjoy creating similar folkloric designs that can be u in either appliquéd or stenciled quilts.

The stenciled quilt is a vital quilt type in our American cultural hist Making stenciled bedcovers and quilts was a popular pastime during first half of the 19th century. The stencil patterns, paints and dyes used fabric were often the same as those used for furniture, walls, floors other home accessories.

While basic stenciling techniques have changed very little through centuries, life is easier for the modern stenciler because special perman fabric paints are available. Also, simplified techniques make stencil easier to do and a lot of fun.

You'll use freezer paper stencils to paint the cardinals and holly, pages 9, 27 and 28), on a whole-cloth background in your version of this quilt.

QUILT SIZE: 41 1/2" x 61 1/2"

MATERIALS
Yardage is estimated for 44" fabric.
• 1 7/8 yards background fabric
• 1 7/8 yards backing fabric
• 46" x 66" piece of batting
• 1/2 yard fabric for binding
• Permanent fabric paints such as DEKA colors in medium green, crimson, orange, black and blue, and extender (a medium that can be mixed with the paints to thin it if necessary)
• Stencil bristle or sponge brushes, one for each color of paint
• Freezer paper
• Craft knife or small, sharp scissors
• Plastic-coated paper plate for paint palette
• Yardstick and pencil for marking fabric

CUTTING
Dimensions include a 1/4" seam allowance.
• Cut 6: 2 1/2" x 44" strips binding fabric

PREPARATION
• Wash the background fabric to remove sizing and press it without using sizing or starch.
• With a yardstick and pencil, center and lightly mark stenciling guidelines on the background fab-

ric, using these dimensions a referring to the diagram: total a of the quilt top- 42" x 62"; bord - 6" wide; blocks (3 across and down) - 10" square. Include diag nal lines, as shown, to help cer the larger design elements wh stenciling the 10" blocks.

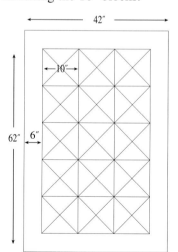

STENCILING PRACTICE
Follow these steps to practice technique and to master the prin ple of painting with freezer pap stencils.
• Cut a 3" square of freezer pap
• With scissors or a craft knife, a simple shape such as a heart o diamond out of the middle of paper. Discard the heart or diamo

The historic look of **"Folkloric Christmas"** *(41 1/2" x 61 1/2") is the result of Nancy Brenan Daniel's interest in traditional American stenciled quilts. Freezer paper stencils make painting on fabric easy and Nancy's choice of fabric for the background is sure to give you ideas for making your own version.*

shape. The remainder is a freeze-paper stencil with which you can paint just the cut-out section and cover the rest of the fabric to protect it from the paint.
• Place this stencil, shiny side down, on a piece of scrap fabric that is cut larger than the stencil. With a warm dry iron, press the stencil to adhere it to the fabric. This keeps the paint from seeping under the paper.
• Place a small amount of paint in any color on the pallette. Work a very small amount of paint into a stencil brush by touching the tips of the bristles in the paint and then rubbing the brush on the palette. Excess paint can be brushed off onto paper towels, if necessary. The

brush should be almost dry when you begin to paint.
• Begin stenciling by brushing the cut-out area in a clockwise motion, starting over the edge of the stencil and bringing the paint onto the fabric. Don't brush toward the edge of the cut-out area because the edges may lift, allowing paint to seep beneath and causing a distorted shape. If you are using a sponge brush, gently tap the paint over the open shape.
   Apply the paint a little at a time. While you can always add more, you can't take it away. If you apply too much paint at one time, it may seep under the stencil and spoil the design.

HINTS
• If you find that the fabric moves around while you are stenciling, place a piece of fine sandpaper under it to help hold it in place.
• Instead of tracing the design several times, make as many photocopies of the original pattern as the number of stencils to be cut. Generally, you'll need one copy of the pattern for each color required in the block or section. However, some design elements in different colors can share the same stencil if they are not too close together. The pattern instructions suggest how many stencils to make. Cut through the photo copy design and freezer paper at the

same time. Because I like to cut two stencils for each motif just in case I ruin one while painting, I layer two pieces of freezer paper under the photocopy for cutting.

• Staple the layers of paper together, outside the design area, for stability while cutting the design.

• Use hole punches in various sizes to cut the small circles.

• Use scissors or a craft knife to cut the paper. Protect the cutting surface under the freezer paper with a cutting mat or cardboard.

• Add dimension and interest to design elements with an accent color. Notice the shading done on the birds and other elements in my quilt.

MAKING THE STENCILS AND PAINTING THE QUILT TOP
Follow these general instructions for all of the stencils used in this quilt. Directions for specific areas follow.

• Place a square of freezer paper on the stencil pattern. (Or photocopy the pattern as per "Hints.") With a pencil, trace the design elements onto freezer paper. Trace only the elements that will be stenciled in the same color. Also make registration marks that indicate the placement of other design elements. These will help you to position the stencils on the fabric properly. Cut out the design elements that will be painted, using a craft knife or small scissors.

• Place a second square of freezer paper over the same pattern and trace the design elements that will be stenciled with another color. For example, if you stencil the bird blocks in the same colors as I did, you'll need to make three stencils—one with the bird and flowers, the second with the stem and leaves, and the third with the large flower centers. Include registration marks and cut out the necessary design elements as before.

• Make the remaining required stencils in the same manner.

• Adhere stencils to the fabric by pressing with a warm, dry iron. Gently peel them up after the paint is dry and reposition them as needed.

Corner Stencils—Make 2 stencils
Stencil pattern on page 28.
• Cut two 6" squares of freezer paper
• Make Stencil 1 - leaves
• Make Stencil 2 - berries in two sizes
• Stencil the quilt top with these, using the pencil guidelines and referring to the quilt photo for placement. Use the corner stencils to paint 8 corner areas, placing the stencils at the intersections of the 10" squares.
• Paint half of this design, "L" fashion,

at each corner of the quilt by taping a piece of scrap paper over the areas of the stencil that don't need to be painted to mask them.

• To create the look of an inner border, paint 3/4 of the corner stencil motif, "T" fashion, at the corners of the 10" squares along the sides of the quilt, masking part of the stencil as before.

Leaf & Berry—Make 1 stencil, use with 2 colors
Stencil pattern on page 27.
• Cut a 3" x 6" rectangle of freezer paper.
• Make the stencil—two leaves, berry.
• To complete the first narrow border, use the stencil to paint the small leaves and berry between the "T" and "L" sections.
Refer to the quilt photo as necessary.

Bird Blocks—Make 3 stencils and 3 reverse stencils
Stencil pattern on page 9.
• Cut six 10" squares of freezer paper
• Place 2 squares of freezer paper shiny sides together and staple them. Repeat, pairing the remaining squares of freezer paper. This will create the reversed images needed for half of the blocks when the stencils are cut.
• Make Stencil 1- bird, berries, flower petals
• Stencil 2 - stems and leaves
• Stencil 3 - centers of large flowers, bird's eye and beak, flower and berry dots
• Paint the stencils in numerical order, centering the design on the fabric in the 10" squares and referring to the quilt photo for placement of reverse images. As you paint, align each stencil with the design elements already painted. Some of the designs may overlap slightly.
• Add shading to design elements as desired. In Stencil 1, the bird and flowers were dry brushed with blue. This shading makes the birds appear to have been stuffed and adds interest to the flowers. In Stencil 2, the holly leaves were dry brushed with red to give them more dimension. In Stencil 3, I shaded the centers of the large flowers with black.

Berry Blocks —Make 2 stencils
Stencil pattern on page 28.
• Cut two 10" squares of freezer paper.
• Make Stencil 1 - green stems, leaves

and small black berries. Trace it on the freezer paper 4 times, rotating the 1/4 pattern 90° and centering the design. Extend 2 of the stems so that they cross the center of the square and connect, as shown.

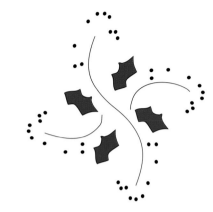

• Make Stencil 2 - red berries.
• Paint the stencils, referring to the quilt photo for placement.

Berry Border—Make 2 stencils
Stencil pattern on page 28.
• Cut two 6" x 10" rectangles of freezer paper.

• Make Stencil 1- green stems, leaves and small black berries.
• Make Stencil 2 - red berries
• Paint the stencils 5 times each along both the top and bottom borders and 8 times on each side border. It's easiest to stencil the motifs at the corners first, and then work toward the center of each border.

FINISHING
• Heat set the fabric paint following the manufacturer's instructions.
• Layer the top, batting and backing fabric. Baste and quilt or tie as desired. My quilt is machine quilted.
• Trim the quilt top to 41 1/2" x 61 1/2".
• Bind the stenciled quilt as described in the *General Directions*, using the 2 1/2" x 44" strips. Don't forget to sign and date your quilt!

———————————————— *QW*

Full-size Bird Block
Stencil Pattern for Folklore Christmas
Stencil patterns are continued on pages 27 and 28.

Hearts at Home

Piece a colorful wallhanging with a country look.

Because of her quilting skills, professional credentials and enthusiasm, Jan Krentz was selected as the 1998 Teacher of the Year by *The Professional Quilter* magazine. Although she has traveled the world, living on Navy bases in Japan and throughout the United States, Jan now calls California home and hundreds of quilters there have benefitted from her classes and lectures. In fact, she's presented workshops in more than three dozen locations in that state alone. Jan has exhibited dozens of her quilts and garments in shows coast to coast and has won first place awards as well as other honors such as Viewer's Choice and fine workmanship awards. Jan has held memberships in several guilds from Virginia to California. She's been a featured artist in a quilt exhibit and made television appearances. Her quilts have been shown in numerous magazines and books. All of these accomplishments stem from her ambition in her high school years. That's when she taught herself to quilt and completed her first project. Jan went on to earn a college degree in interior design from the University of Nebraska. Her teaching career began in 1988 when Jan offered private quilting lessons in her home. Her specialties are many. Jan teaches classes in stenciling, foundation piecing, machine quilting, trapunto, appliqué, photo transfer and fabric dyeing. Her popular Danish Hearts pattern is featured in "Hearts at Home."

Contact information:
Jan Krentz, 9048 Twin Trails Ct.,
San Diego, CA 92129-2523
E-mail: jpkrentz@worldnet.att.net
Website: http;//home.att.net/~jpkrentz/

Danish Heart blocks set on point form the central medallion of this charming quilt. Tiny foundation-pieced hearts in the sashing have a three-dimensional look made by folding a square to form the "V" and catching it in the final seam. The four foundation-pieced houses are placed in the corners on their hilly landscapes. I chose fabrics for cheerful red doors and golden windows to reflect the happy families inside!

Measure, cut and piece carefully when making your version of "Hearts at Home." Press seams gently to avoid stretching pieces out of shape. Measure when you are ready to assemble the hearts and sashing, ensuring that the blocks are all the same size to keep the central medallion in square. You'll need to custom-fit the corner segments which include House blocks, Flying Geese strips and "landscape" units to fit your center medallion. My directions call for making foundations and pattern pieces for the corner sections using freezer paper.

QUILT SIZE: 39 1/2" square
BLOCK SIZE: 7 1/2" square

MATERIALS
Yardage is estimated for 44" fabric.
- Up to 9 fat quarters (18" x 22") light prints, for the Danish Heart blocks
- Up to 9 fat quarters medium to dark prints, for the Danish Heart blocks and cornerstones
- 1 1/2 yards light print for the background in Danish Heart blocks, sashing and cornerstones NOTE: *If you prefer a scrappier look, choose a variety of light-value fat quarters for the blocks and 1/2 yard for the sashing.*
- Assorted print scraps for the House blocks
- 4 fat quarters medium to light background prints for the House blocks and corner sections
- Assorted colorful print scraps for the "geese"
- Assorted light print scraps for the background of the Flying Geese
- 1/2 yard dark print for the binding
- 1 1/4 yards backing fabric
- 44" square of batting
- Freezer paper
- Fine-line permanent black marking pen such as a Sharpie®

CUTTING
Dimensions include a 1/4" seam allowance. Fabric for foundation piecing will be cut as you sew the blocks and units. Each piece should be at least 1/2" larger on all sides than the section it will cover. Refer to the General Directions as needed.
For each of 9 Danish Heart blocks:
Pair a light and a dark print fabric. Decide which of them is Fabric A and which is Fabric B. You'll cut more squares from Fabric B than from Fabric A for the Nine Patch unit in the block.
- Cut 4: 2" squares, Fabric A
- Cut 1: 3 1/2" x 5" rectangle, Fabric A
- Cut 5: 2" squares, Fabric B
- Cut 1: 3 1/2" x 5" rectangle, Fabric B
- Cut 4: 2" squares, light background print
- Cut 1: 3 1/2" square, light background print
Also:
- Cut 24: 2" x 8" strips, light background print for sashing
- Cut 16: 1 1/2" squares, light background print for cornerstone piecing NOTE: *If you prefer, cut sixteen 2" medium or dark print squares to use for cornerstones instead of foundation piecing them.*

"Hearts at Home" (39 1/2" square) by Jan Krentz of San Diego, California, contains Danish Heart blocks, foundation-pieced Houses and cornerstones, and custom-made corner sections. Photo by Carina Woolrich.

• Cut 5: 2 1/2" x 44" strips, dark print for the binding

PIECING

For each Danish Heart block:

• Lay out the 2" Fabric A and B squares to form a Nine Patch unit, as shown. 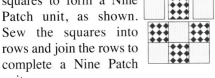 Sew the squares into rows and join the rows to complete a Nine Patch unit.

• Mark a diagonal line on the wrong side of each 2" light background print square.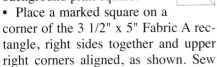

• Place a marked square on a corner of the 3 1/2" x 5" Fabric A rectangle, right sides together and upper right corners aligned, as shown. Sew

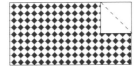

on the marked line. Fold the light square over the seamline toward the corner and press. Trim away the two layers beneath the light print triangle 1/4" beyond the seamline.

• In the same manner, place a marked square on the opposite corner of the Fabric A rectangle, as shown. Sew on the line. Open, press and trim as before to complete a Fabric A Heart unit.

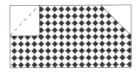

• Using the remaining marked squares and the 3 1/2" x 5" Fabric B rectangle, make a Fabric B Heart unit in the same manner.

• Lay out the Fabric A and B Heart units, the Nine Patch unit and the 3 1/2" light background square, as shown. Sew the units into pairs and join the pairs to complete a Danish Heart block. Make 9.

For the cornerstones:

Follow the foundation piecing instructions in the General Directions *to piece the cornerstones. Use a dry iron on a cotton setting and avoid touching the shiny surface of the freezer paper with the iron when pressing.*

- Trace the foundation pattern for the cornerstones (page 13) on the dull side of freezer paper 16 times, transferring all lines and numbers and leaving a 1" space between foundations. Cut each one out 1/2" beyond the broken line.
- Use the following fabrics in these positions:

1 - dark or medium print

2, 3 - light background print

4 - 1 1/2" square of light background print folded in quarters; pin the folded square in place to secure it, keeping raw edges aligned with the edges of the foundation. Do not sew it yet.

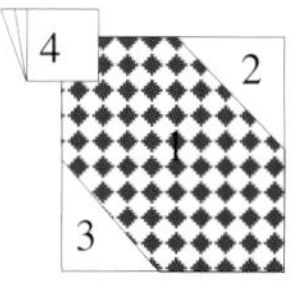

5 - light background (Remove the pin from the three-dimensional #4 piece as you stitch the position 5 fabric in place. This seam will secure the #4 piece. Trim the seam allowance of the #4 piece after stitching to reduce bulk.)
- Baste each foundation in the seam allowance, halfway between the stitching line and the broken line, to hold fabrics in place, if desired.
- Trim each foundation on the broken line.

For the House blocks:
- Trace the House sections (A-F on pages 13 and 17) 4 times each on the dull side of freezer paper. Cut them out as before and foundation piece each section, referring to the *General Directions* as needed.

For each Section A:
- Use the following fabrics in these positions:

1 - chimney print

2, 3, 4 - background print

For each Section B:
- Use the following fabrics in these positions:

1 - chimney print

2, 3 - background print

For each Section C:
- Use the following fabrics in these positions:

1 - house print, placed on the bias

2 - roof print

3, 4 - background print

For each Section D:
- Use the following fabrics in positions:

1 - window print

2 through 4 - house print

5 - house print, placed on the bias

6 - door print

7 - house print, placed on the bias

For each Section E:
- Use the following fabrics in these positions:

1 - window print

2, 3 - house print

For each Section F:
- Use the following fabrics in these positions:

1 - sidewalk print

2, 3 - grass print
- Baste each section to hold fabrics in place, if desired, and trim as before.
- Referring to the Block Diagram, join the appropriate sections to complete a House block. Make 4. Set them aside.

- Lay out the Danish Heart blocks, 2" x 8" light background print sashing strips and pieced cornerstones, referring to the quilt photo as needed. Sew them into diagonal rows and join the rows to complete the center medallion.

For the Corner Sections:
- Cut a large piece of freezer paper on which to draw a corner section. This will be used for the pattern pieces, so draw carefully.
- Lay the center medallion on point on a flat work surface, right side up. Place freezer paper, dull side up, next to one side of the center medallion, edges touching. Tape the center medallion and the freezer paper to the table. With a pencil and ruler, draw a right triangle on the freezer paper in the size that will square up your quilt, having a 90° angle at the outer corner and 45° angles at each corner of the center medallion. Both sides of the triangle should be equal in length. Center and draw a 7 1/2" square in the triangle where

the House block will be placed. Extend the lawn by drawing triangles, as shown in the diagram. Then draw areas where the Flying Geese borders and the corner square will be.

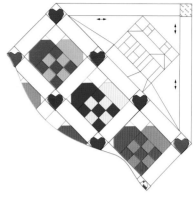

- When the corner section drawing is complete, go over the pencil lines with the permanent pen. Use a ruler to make the lines straight.
- Use a ruler and a rotary cutter (fitted with a blade you use for paper) to cut apart the corner section on the marked lines. Label the pieces left-side grass, left-side background, right-side grass, right-side background, top triangle, corner square and geese units. Mark grainlines on the triangles to keep fabric straight of grain on the outside edges.
- Divide one of the Flying Geese strips evenly by folding the strip in half repeatedly, creating equal-size sections. Open the strip and mark the folds using the permanent pen and a ruler. Fold the section in half lengthwise to crease a center line. Draw stitching lines from the edge of the paper at each fold to the center line to create triangles.
- Using this Flying Geese section as a guide, cut 8 strips of freezer paper this size, adding 1/4" on all sides for seam allowances. Center the guide beneath one of these strips of freezer paper and transfer the marks for sewing lines with the permanent pen. Repeat with the remaining freezer paper strips.
- Piece the Flying Geese on the freezer paper foundations, starting at the bottom of each strip. Place fabric on the unmarked side and stitch on the marked side. See foundation piecing directions in the *General Directions*.

• Set aside the 7 1/2" square of freezer paper that represents the House blocks for another project.
• Press the freezer paper patterns for the top triangle, the corner square, the left-and right-side grass triangles, and the left- and right-side background triangles on the right side of the appropriate fabrics. Cut them out, adding 1/4" seam allowances on each side.
• Remove the patterns from these fabrics and re-use them to cut pieces for the three remaining corner sections.
• Sew a left-side grass triangle and left-side background triangle together to make a left-side unit. Make 4.
• Sew a right-side grass triangle and right-side background triangle together to make a right-side unit. Make 4.

• Lay out a House block, top triangle, left-side unit, right-side unit, Flying Geese strips and corner square for one corner section. Sew them together to complete a corner section. Make 4.
• Center and pin a corner section to one side of the center medallion, pinning seam intersections. Sew the seam, easing in any fullness as necessary. Sew corner sections to the remaining sides of the center medallion to complete the quilt top.
• Remove the paper foundations and finish the quilt as described in the *General Directions*, using the 2 1/2" x 44" dark print strips for the binding.

— *QW*

Full-size Foundation Pattern for Cornerstones

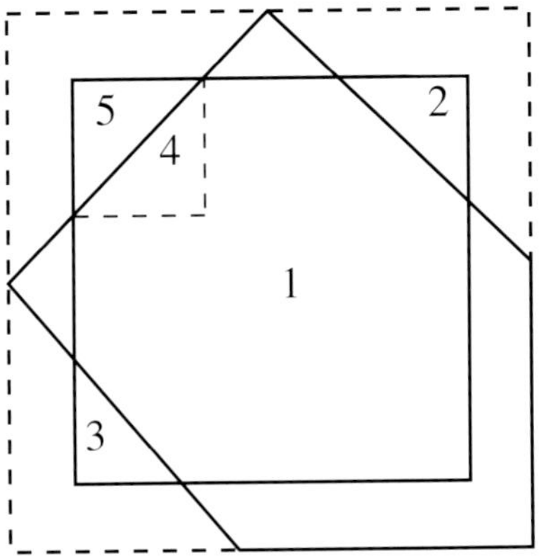

Full-size Foundation Patterns for Hearts at Home

continued on page 17

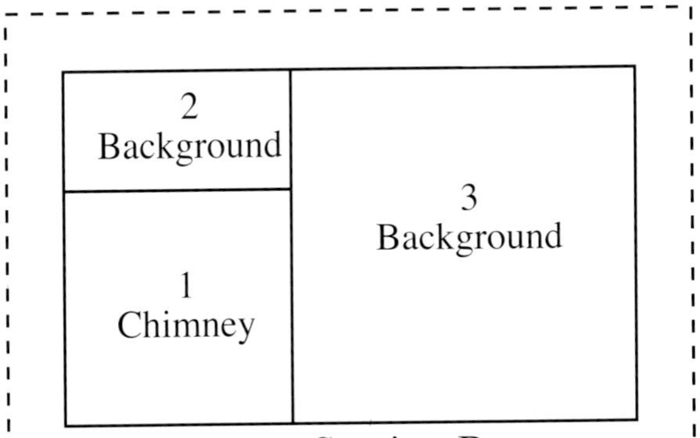

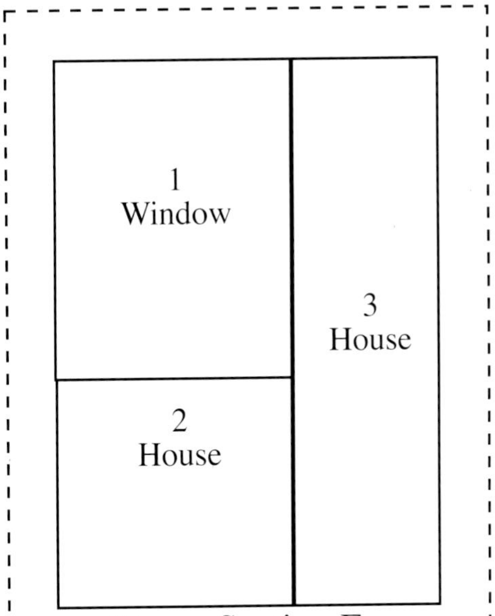

House Section E

House Section B

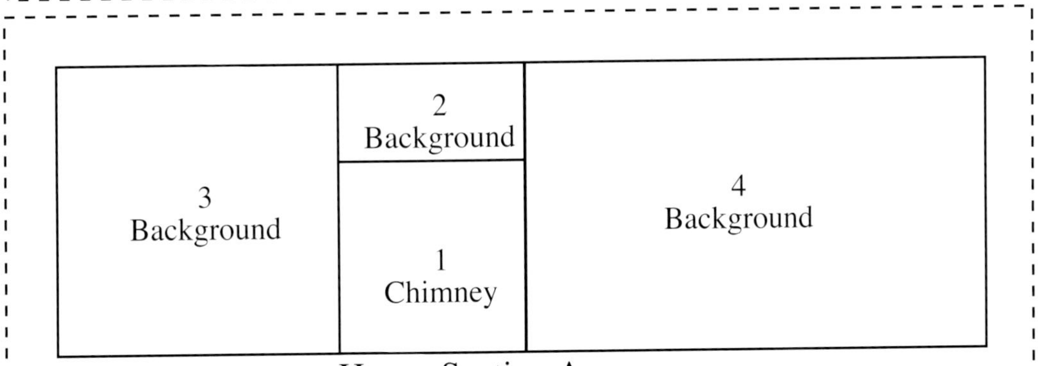

House Section A

Madison House Gets a New Look

Piece a delightful "village" without templates!

Truly a "dynamic duo" in the quilt world, California teachers Laura Nownes (right) and Diana McClun (left) have co-authored several best-selling quilt books. Their first, *Quilts! Quilts!! Quilts!!!* (2nd edition, 1997, Quilt Digest Press), began as a series of handouts they prepared for a basic quiltmaking class. With the addition of colorful quilt photos and diagrams, the handout became a quilting manual that quilters have relied on since it was first published in 1988. Diana hails from a long line of quiltmakers and has a degree in Home Economics. She opened a quilt shop called Empty Spools where she met Laura, a student in several beginning quilting classes. Laura's skills progressed rapidly and she eventually became the store manager, teaching basic classes herself. The partners went on to collaborate on quilts and another book from Quilt Digest Press, *Quilts Galore,* as well as two books from C&T Publishing, *Say it With Quilts* and *Quilts, Quilts and More Quilts.* Today, they continue to teach throughout the United States, both together and separately. Each woman brings unique talents to their partnership. Diana is credited with color expertise while Laura's focus is the technical aspect of their designs. They work color magic in their updated "Madison House" quilt made with easy construction methods.

Contact information:
Diana McClun/Laura Nownes,
70 Bradley Ave., Walnut Creek, CA 94596

M any of our students love house quilts and enjoyed the original "Madison House" quilt in our first book, *Quilts! Quilts!! Quilts!!!* We updated the pattern for our revised edition, making it look more like a village in springtime. We added tree blocks, chose a different background fabric for each row and rotary cut all of the pieces.

We also used an easy construction method for piecing the roofs and trees without triangles. Here's how to create the angled seams in each of the pieces:

• For the roof, place a background square at each end of a roof rectangle, right sides together. Stitch across each square diagonally in the direction shown. Trim the excess fabric 1/4" beyond the seamline, open the background fabric and press to complete the pieced roof section.

• Similarly, sew background pieces to each end of the tree rectangles. The only difference is that you'll be sewing different size rectangles for Rows 1 and 2 and squares for Row 3. Refer to these diagrams as needed when piecing the blocks. HELPFUL HINT: *Press the angles on the background pieces before sewing.*

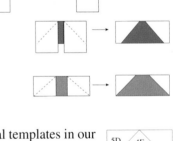

Each of the blocks has a labeled diagram to guide you when selecting fabrics. The numbers and letters refer to pattern pieces for traditional templates in our book. They are used here to help you keep track of the pieces while you sew, even though you'll be rotary cutting the pieces. Notice that within each House block in our quilt, chimneys match. Also, upstairs and downstairs verandahs are cut from 1"-wide strips of the same fabric. In addition to the backgrounds, some pieces such as chimneys, doors and verandahs also match within rows. You may want to keep this in mind when selecting fabrics and deciding how scrappy you want your quilt to be.

The border is made from 3 1/2" units cut from 1 1/2"-wide cut and pieced strips. These are made using the four background fabrics and assorted dark prints. You can randomly mix units when piecing the borders or shade them from dark to light, matching the rows as we did. So pick out some wonderful fabrics and stitch your own version of "Madison House."

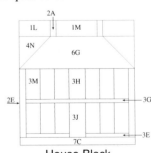

House Block

"Madison House" *(73" x 67") has grown into a small community in this updated version of a design by Diana McClun and Laura Nownes. Rotary cutting, strip piecing and an easy construction method for the angled pieces in the roofs and trees make this quilt quick to stitch. This quilt is featured in* Quilts! Quilts!! Quilts!!! *2nd edition. Machine quilted by Kathy Sandbach. Photo by Sharon Risedorph*

QUILT SIZE: 73" x 67"
BLOCK SIZE: 12" square House block, 6" x 12" Tree block

MATERIALS
Yardage is estimated for 44" fabric.
• 3/4 yard each of 4 background prints
NOTE: *We chose fabrics that range from medium-dark to light values. If you wish to shade your border to match the rows, purchase 1 yard each of the darkest and lightest fabrics.*
• Assorted print and solid scraps to total 3 yards for the houses
• Assorted print scraps to total 1/2 yard for the trees
• Assorted dark print scraps to total 5/8 yard for the pieced border
NOTE: *The border is sewn using units cut from pieced strips. Be sure these scraps are at least 22" long so*
you can cut several units from them.
• 2 yards floral print for the horizontal sashing (cut lengthwise)
• 4 yards of backing fabric
• 77" x 71" piece of batting
• 5/8 yard dark print for the binding

CUTTING
Dimensions include a 1/4" seam allowance. Group and label the pieces for each block as you cut them to identify them by row.
For the 16 House blocks:
• Cut 32: 1 1/2" x 6 1/2" rectangles, background prints, 8 from each print (2E)
• Cut 32: 2 1/2" x 3 1/2" rectangles, background prints, 8 from each print (1L)
• Cut 16: 2 1/2" x 4 1/2" rectangles, background prints, 4 from each print (1M)

• Cut 32: 3 1/2" squares, background prints, 8 from each print (4N)
• Cut 32: 1 1/2" x 2 1/2" rectangles in matching sets of 2, assorted scraps, for the chimneys (2A)
• Cut 16: 3 1/2" x 12 1/2" rectangles, assorted scraps, for the roofs (6G)
• Cut 8: 1" x 44" strips, dark fabric, for the verandahs; from them cut thirty-two 1" x 4 5/8" strips (3E) and sixteen 1" x 10 1/2" strips (3G)
• Cut 32: 1 7/8" x 16" strips in matching sets of 2, assorted prints, for the house fronts (3M)
• Cut 16: 1 7/8" x 16" strips, assorted prints, for the windows (also 3M)
• Cut 16: 1 1/2" x 12 1/2" strips, assorted prints, for the ground (7C)
• Cut 16: 2 1/4" x 3" rectangles, assorted prints, for the upstairs doors (3H)
• Cut 16: 2 1/4" x 3 1/2" rectangles,

assorted prints, for the downstairs doors (3J)

For the 12 Tree blocks:
- Cut 24: 2 1/2" x 3 1/2" rectangles, background prints, 6 from each print (5D)
- Cut 24: 2 1/2" x 3" rectangles, background prints, 6 from each print (5C)
- Cut 24: 2 1/2" squares, background prints, 6 from each print (4P)
- Cut 24: 3" x 6 1/2" rectangles, background prints, 6 from each print (3L)
- Cut 12: 2 1/2" x 4 1/2" rectangles, assorted scraps, for the trees (4F)
- Cut 12: 2 1/2" x 5 1/2" rectangles, assorted scraps, for the trees (5F)
- Cut 12: 2 1/2" x 6 1/2" rectangles, assorted scraps, for the trees (5E)
- Cut 12: 1 1/2" x 6 1/2" rectangles, assorted scraps, for the tree trunks (2E)

Also:
- Cut 4: 3 1/2" x 66 1/2" lengthwise strips, floral print, for horizontal sashing
- Cut 24: 1 1/2" x 22" strips, assorted dark prints, for pieced borders
- Cut 24: 1 1/2" x 22" strips, background prints, for pieced borders
NOTE: *These are sewn into pieced sets and cut into units for the pieced border. If you wish to match the background print used in the border to that used in each adjacent row, you'll need to cut 9 strips each from the darkest and lightest background prints and 3 strips from each of the remaining background prints.*
- Cut 8: 1 7/8" x 44" strips, dark print, for the binding

DIRECTIONS
For the House blocks:
- Make a chimney section by sewing together two matching 2 1/2" x 3 1/2" background print rectangles (1L), two 1 1/2" x 2 1/2" chimney rectangles (2A) and a matching 2 1/2" x 4 1/2" background print rectangle (1M), as shown.

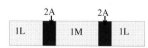

- Make a roof section by sewing matching 3 1/2" background print squares (4N) to opposite ends of a 3 1/2" x 12 1/2" roof rectangle (6G). Refer to the roof diagrams and the stitching directions on page 14.
- Sew a 1 7/8" x 16" window strip between matching 1 7/8" x 16" house strips, right sides together along their length, to make a pieced set. Cut four

3" units from the pieced set.

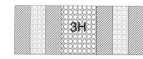

- Sew a 2 1/4" x 3" upstairs door rectangle (3H) between two of the units to make an upstairs section, as shown.

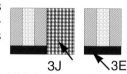

- Sew 1" x 4 5/8" dark verandah strips (3E) to the remaining two units to make downstairs window sections.
- Sew a 2 1/4" x 3 1/2" downstairs door rectangle (3J) between the two window sections to make a downstairs section, as shown.

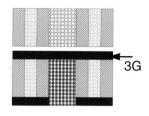

- Sew a 1" x 10 1/2" dark verandah strip (3G) between the upstairs and downstairs sections to make a house front.

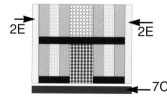

- Sew matching 1 1/2" x 6 1/2" background print rectangles (2E) to opposite sides of the house front.
- Sew a 1 1/2" x 12 1/2" ground strip (7C) to the bottom of the house front to complete a house section.

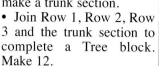

- Join the chimney, roof and house sections to complete a House block. Make 16. Group them in four piles of four blocks, according to the background fabric used.

For the Tree blocks:
- Referring to the tree diagrams and stitching directions on page 14, piece three tree rows using these pieces: Row 1 - two matching 2 1/2" x 3 1/2" background print rectangles (5D) and a 2 1/2" x 4 1/2" tree rectangle (4F); Row 2 - two matching 2 1/2" x 3" background print rectangles (5C) and a 2 1/2" x 5 1/2" tree rectangle (5F);

Row 3 - two matching 2 1/2" background print squares (4P) and a 2 1/2" x 6 1/2" tree rectangle (5E).
- Sew a 1 1/2" x 6 1/2" tree rectangle (2E) between two matching 3" x 6 1/2" background print rectangles (3L), to make a trunk section.
- Join Row 1, Row 2, Row 3 and the trunk section to complete a Tree block. Make 12.

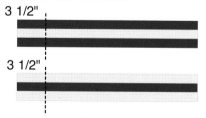

- Group the Tree blocks in four piles of three blocks, according to the background print used. Place each pile with the pile of House blocks made using the corresponding background print. Each pile of 7 blocks will be used in one row.
- Lay out the blocks in horizontal rows, placing them in an arrangement you like or referring to the quilt photo for block placement. Sew the blocks into rows.
- Sew a 3 1/2" x 66 1/2" floral print strip to the bottom of each row. Join the rows.

To make the pieced border:
- Sew a 1 1/2" x 22" background print strip between two 1 1/2" x 22" dark print strips, right sides together along their length, to make a dark pieced strip. Make 8.
- Sew a 1 1/2" x 22" dark print strip between two matching 1 1/2" x 22" background print strips, right sides together along their length, to make a light pieced strip. Make 8.
- Cut 3 1/2" units from each pieced set. You will need 88 units.

- Alternating light and dark units and referring to the quilt photo as necessary, join 20 units to make a side border. Make 2. Join 24 units each for the top and bottom borders.

FINISHING
- Sew pieced borders to the sides of the quilt top.
- Sew pieced borders to the top and bottom of the quilt top.
- Finish the quilt as described in the *General Directions*, using the 1 7/8" x 44" dark print strips for the binding.

QW

Hearts at Home

(continued from page 13)

Full-size Foundation Patterns for Hearts at Home
Directions begin on page 10.

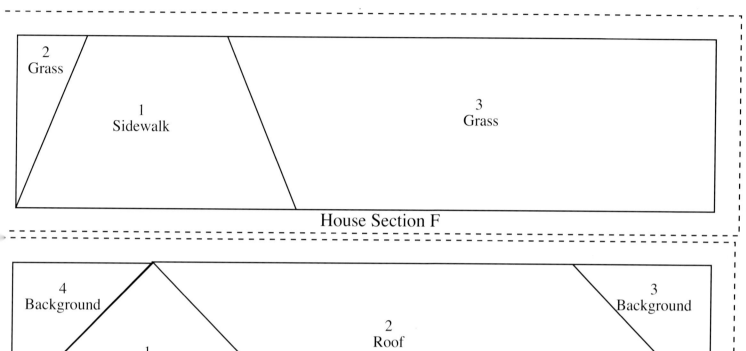

House Section F

House Section C

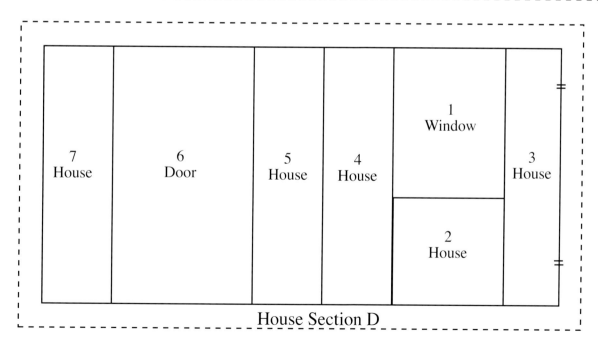

House Section D

String-Pieced Star

Learn a tried-and-true technique while you make this easy wallhanging.

The string-pieced quilt is one that has been a part of our quilting heritage for well over 100 years. For quite some time quiltmakers have stitched long narrow strips or "strings" of fabric together on a foundation to make quilts in many designs. The strings were often strips of fabric left over from home sewing, garment factory cut-aways, recycled strips from used clothing or strips left from other quiltmaking projects. By making quilts of these fabric strings, women were using what they had so they could make warm bed coverings for their families and beautify their homes. Gather your fabric scraps and try your hand at this popular '30s technique.

With a love for vintage quilts, teacher and quilt historian Beverly Dunivent has developed her quilting specialty. Beverly makes reproduction quilts (ones made to resemble antiques) reminiscent of the 1930s. Often dressed in period costume, she teaches classes and gives lectures on Depression-era quilts. Beverly lives in a rural and mountainous area of California where she quilts in her large studio. From there, she travels throughout the United States, teaching and lecturing. As an American Quilter's Society (AQS) certified appraiser, she also determines the value of quilts. Beverly's workshops include machine quilting, autograph quilts, contemporary scrap quilts and foundation piecing. She also conducts a class on rescuing vintage blocks and incorporating them in quilt projects while another class focuses on how to care for and repair antique quilts. Beverly's articles have appeared in numerous magazines, including *Traditional Quiltworks*. She has served as guest curator for several antique quilt exhibits. For more than two decades Beverly has honed her quilting skills and expertise. She now is a consultant to RJR Fabrics for their line of 1930s reproduction prints. Beverly's colorful quilts made using string piecing (a popular technique of the '30s) are scrappy and authentic looking. Beverly shares the method and a pattern in her "String-pieced Star."

Contact information:
Beverly Dunivent, P.O. Box 8517,
Green Valley Lake, CA 92341
E-mail: bevquilt@sprynet.com

QUILT SIZE: 32 1/2" x 36"

MATERIALS
• Assorted fat quarters and scraps of 1930s reproduction prints and solids. Include light, medium and dark. I like to use a wide selection—25 or more fabrics.
• 2 1/2 yards of fabric for the background, outer border, backing and binding—I chose black for high contrast
• 37" x 40" piece of batting
• Paper for the foundations. Freezer paper, copier paper or typing paper work well.

CUTTING
Dimensions include a 1/4" seam allowance.
• Cut strips of prints and solids in various widths from 1 1/2" to 3". These "strings" can be cut quickly, without thought to making them perfectly straight. You can angle strips as you sew to add visual interest to the quilt.
• Mix the strings in a see-through plastic container and study them to be sure the mix is appealing. The more fabrics you use, the richer your quilt will look.
• Cut 12: Paper foundations using the triangle pattern on page 29. Stack the paper and cut several foundations at once using a rotary cutter with an old blade.
• Cut 4: 2" x 30" paper foundations for the inner border
• Cut 4: 3" x 33" strips, fabric for

the outer border
• Cut 4: 2 1/2" x 44" strips, fabric for the binding
• Cut 1: 37" x 40" piece of backing fabric

DIRECTIONS
Piecing the units:
• Place one strip of fabric, right side up, across the center of a foundation paper triangle. Trim the strip so that it extends approximately 1/2" beyond the edges of the paper.
• Place a second strip on the first one, right sides together, and stitch, angling the second strip for interest if you wish. To angle a strip, sew it so that its edges aren't even with the previous one.

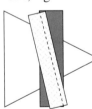

Flip the second strip open. If you angle a strip, the shape of the previous strip will be altered when the second strip is flipped open. Study the quilt photo to see where strips have been angled.
• Sew a third strip to the opposite side of the first one, angling it for interest as desired.
• Trim the excess fabric from both seam allowances to reduce bulk.
• Press the string-pieced section from the right side.

Beverly Dunivent made this striking **"String-Pieced Star"** *(32 1/2" x 36") entirely by machine for a fast and fun project. She selected black for the background and borders after seeing photos of interesting vintage '30s quilts that were made with large amounts of black fabric.*

• Continue adding strips to cover the foundation, trimming and pressing each time a strip is added to both sides. For the last strip at each end of the foundation, select a wide one in order to avoid the bulk of multiple seams in the corners. You'll find it easier when setting the string-pieced units together.

• Press the finished unit and trim it even with the edges of the foundation. Leave the paper in place for now. Make 12.

• Lay out the string-pieced units to form a six-pointed star, referring to the Assembly Diagram and the quilt photo for direction of strips. Stitch the units into rows and join the rows to complete the star. NOTE: *Stop and backstitch 1/4" from the edges of the six seam intersections where background pieces will be set in.* Press the seam allowances open.

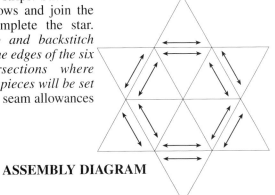

ASSEMBLY DIAGRAM

Making templates for setting pieces:

• Lay the star on a large sheet of freezer paper. You'll need to make the two templates shown in the diagram to cut setting pieces from the background fabric.

• For template A, measure and draw horizontal lines 2" out from the star points at the two locations shown in the diagram. Mark dots at these two points. Use your ruler to draw lines connecting the star points and dots and a vertical line connecting the dots. Then trace the two edges of the star indicated in the diagram in order to complete template A. Remove the star and add a 1/4"

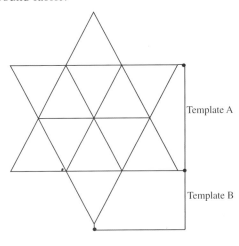

Template A

Template B

(Continued on page 29)

California Rail

Create a dynamic quilt with lots of fabrics and easy stitching!

California quiltmaker Mary Ellen Hopkins is well known in the quilt world for her energy and wit. She uses it to punctuate lectures and classes based on her traditional yet lively quilt designs. A longtime seamstress, Mary Ellen began her quilting career when she opened a shop called Crazy Ladies and Friends. Over the years, she developed streamlined piecing techniques that made it possible to achieve a complex-looking design in a short amount of time. Mary Ellen also designed quilts using simple block patterns in new ways, turning the blocks into originals. She shares her piecing methods along with her design approach in classes and books. *It's Okay if You Sit on My Quilt, A Log Cabin Notebook, Connecting Up, …Continuing On, Kansas Connections* and *Even More Well Connected* are some of Mary Ellen's books that explore quilt designs and include her quick-piecing methods. All are published by ME Publications. Mary Ellen eventually sold her quilt shop to focus on writing, traveling and teaching. She currently offers quilting seminars for teachers and shop owners and continues to make exciting quilts like the "California Rail" presented here.

Contact information:
Mary Ellen Hopkins, ME Publications,
P.O. Box 1288, Cardiff By the Sea, CA 92007
Website: www.maryellenhopkins.com

Are you familiar with the Rail Fence pattern? Typically, it's a block stitched using three or more contrasting fabric rectangles. If a dark fabric is used on one side of the block and the blocks are placed in alternating directions when they're joined, a striking zig-zag design moves across the quilt top.

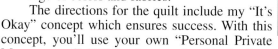

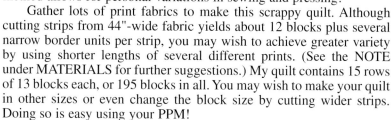

In my easy "California Rail" quilt, an updated variation of the Rail Fence pattern, you can achieve the same look but with less sewing! When you use many different prints, you can also explore the effects of color while arranging the blocks. I've included a diagram for one possible arrangement, but I'm sure you'll think of more. As you study the photo of my quilt, notice the range of colors and fabrics.

The directions for the quilt include my "It's Okay" concept which ensures success. With this concept, you'll use your own "Personal Private Measurement" (PPM) when cutting blocks from pieced strips. You'll measure the width of strip-pieced panels that you sew together to determine your PPM. Your accuracy can't miss because this measuring method allows for personal variations in sewing and pressing!

Gather lots of print fabrics to make this scrappy quilt. Although cutting strips from 44"-wide fabric yields about 12 blocks plus several narrow border units per strip, you may wish to achieve greater variety by using shorter lengths of several different prints. (See the NOTE under MATERIALS for further suggestions.) My quilt contains 15 rows of 13 blocks each, or 195 blocks in all. You may wish to make your quilt in other sizes or even change the block size by cutting wider strips. Doing so is easy using your PPM!

QUILT SIZE: Approximately 38" x 43"

BLOCK SIZE: Approximately 2 1/2"—Your Personal Private Measurement will determine the exact size

MATERIALS
Yardage is estimated for 44" fabric.

• Assorted prints totaling about 1 yard
NOTE: *You'll cut 2 1/4"-wide strips from these. Various lengths will work. For example, when pieced, a 22"-long strip will yield five blocks plus three narrower border units. You can include more than 30 prints in your quilt working with strips this length. For even greater variety, cut 18"-long* strips from 50 prints. When pieced an 18"-long strip will yield four blocks plus two or three border units.

• 1 yard black
• 1 1/2 yards red print
NOTE: *You will cut lengthwise strips from this for the inner border. Cut these strips after completing and measuring the quilt center.*
• 2 1/2 yards backing fabric
• 42" x 47" piece of batting

CUTTING
Dimensions include a 1/4" seam allowance.
• Cut 2 1/4"-wide strips in various lengths from the prints
• Cut 15: 1 1/4" x 44" strips, black
• Cut 5: 2 1/2" x 44" strips, black for the binding

Do you love the scrappy look? Do you love quilts that can be made quickly using easy strip-piecing methods? Then this **"California Rail"** *(38" x 43") is for you! Popular teacher Mary Ellen Hopkins is known for simplifying designs without compromising their creative impact. This quilt works up so fast that you may want to make more than one! Photo courtesy of ME Publications.*

DIRECTIONS

• Sew a 1 1/4"-wide black strip to a 2 1/4"-wide print strip, right sides together along their length, to make a pieced strip. Trim the excess from the black strip and set it aside to use with another print strip.

• Working from the right side, press the seam allowance toward the black strip.

• Repeat to make pieced strips, using the remaining black and print strips.

• Measure the width of a pieced strip from raw edge to raw edge. This is your "Personal Private Measurement" (PPM)—the measurement you'll use to slice blocks from the pieced strips.

3"

Record this measurement. It will be approximately 3", depending on your sewing and pressing.

• Cut blocks that are the same size as your PPM from each pieced strip, reserving some of the pieced strips for cutting border units later. Cut a total of 195 blocks.

• Lay out the blocks in 15 rows of 13, creating an arrangement that pleases you and alternating the placement of the black strip to achieve the zig-zag design. Refer to the quilt photo and Suggested Layout Diagram.

SUGGESTED LAYOUT DIAGRAM

(Continued on page 30)

Autumn Pines

"Landscape" your Log Cabin blocks with a Pine Tree border.

Oregon native Jean Wells has inspired thousands of quilters in her long quilting career. She opened her quilt shop, the Stitchin' Post, in Sisters, Oregon, 25 years ago. If that place sounds familiar, perhaps it's because you've attended or seen photos of a famous annual outdoor event known as the Sisters Oregon Quilt Show. Jean conceived the idea for the exhibit and directs it each year. The first of Jean's more than two dozen books was written in 1979. Each of her books contains photos of her beautiful quilts along with patterns and hints to make sewing them easy. Jean's goal is to bring out the creativity in each of her students and to develop their skills by providing thorough instructions and easy techniques. Her projects range from traditional to folk-art. In addition to quilting, Jean loves gardening and many floral quilts appear in her books, including a book titled *Everything Flowers: Quilts from the Garden*. Other book titles include *Patchwork Quilts Made Easy*, *No-Sew Appliqué*, *Buttonhole Stitch Appliqué*, *Memorabilia Quilting*, and *Willowood*. Jean collaborated with her daughter Valori, a talented photographer, in writing *Everything Flowers: Quilts from the Garden* and *Through the Garden Gate* for C&T Publishing. As a designer for P&B Textiles, Jean brings to market the types of fabric quilters want. Her "Autumn Pines" quilt features easy chain piecing and quick methods for Log Cabin and Tree blocks. This project also appears in *Patchwork Quilts Made Easy* by Jean Wells (C&T Publishing) and is reprinted with permission of the author and publisher.

Contact information:
Jean Wells, c/o C&T Publishing,
1651 Challenge Drive, Concord, CA 94520-5206

When you make this classic design, you'll practice subcutting fabric pieces for the Log Cabin blocks and Tree border from selvage-to-selvage strips. You'll also try an easy method for making double half-square triangles. These units have many uses in quiltmaking as seen in the Tree border.

QUILT SIZE: 82 1/2" x 94 1/2"
BLOCK SIZE: 11 1/4" square

MATERIALS
- Assorted dark fabrics for the Log Cabin blocks, totaling 3 1/2 yards
- Assorted light fabrics for the Log Cabin blocks, totaling 3 1/4 yards
- 1 yard gold print for the background of the Tree border.
- 7/8 yard rust for the Log Cabin block centers and inner border
- Assorted dark greens for the Tree border, totaling 1 1/8 yards
- 1/2 yard dark green for the binding
- 1/8 yard brown for the tree trunks
- 5 1/2 yards backing fabric
- 87" x 99" piece of batting

CUTTING
The usable width of fabric is usually about 42", so that dimension is used for selvage-to-selvage strips. The patches in each block are lettered (see diagrams). I recommend using sticky notes to label each stack of patches. All dimensions include a 1/4" seam allowance.

For the Log Cabin blocks:
- Cut 66: 1 3/4" x 42" strips, assorted dark fabrics. From them, cut 42 logs in each of the following lengths: 3" (D), 4 1/4" (E), 5 1/2" (H), 6 3/4" (I), 8" (L), 9 1/4" (M), 10 1/2" (P) and 11 3/4" (Q).
- Cut 54: 1 3/4" x 42" strips, assorted light fabrics. From them, cut 42 logs in each of the following lengths: 1 3/4"

(B), 3" (C), 4 1/4" (F), 5 1/2" (G), 6 3/4" (J), 8" (K), 9 1/4" (N), and 10 1/2" (O).
- Cut 2: 1 3/4" x 42" strips, red. From them, cut forty-two 1 3/4" center squares (A).

For the Tree Border:
- Cut 6: 2 1/2" x 42" strips, dark green. From them, cut fifty-two 2 1/2" x 4 1/2" rectangles (A).
- Cut 9: 2 1/2" x 42" strips, dark green. From them, cut fifty-two 2 1/2" x 6 1/2" rectangles (C).
- Cut 13: 2 1/2" x 42" strips, gold print. From them, cut two hundred eight 2 1/2" squares (B and D).
- Cut 7: 1 1/2" x 42" strips, gold print. From them, cut forty-eight 1 1/2" x 5 3/4" rectangles (E).
- Cut 3: 2 1/2" x 42" strips, gold print. From them, cut forty-eight 2 1/2" squares (G).
- Cut 1: 1 1/2" x 42" strip, gold print. From it, cut eight 1 1/2" x 3 1/8" rectangles (H).
- Cut 1: 2 1/2" x 42" strip, gold print. From it, cut eight 1 1/2" x 2 1/2" rectangles (I).
- Cut 2: 1 1/2" x 42" strips, brown. From them, cut fifty-two 1 1/4" x 1 1/2" rectangles (F).

Also:
- Cut 4: 2 3/4" x 42" strips, red, for the inner border (sides)
- Cut 4: 3 1/8" x 42" strips, red, for the inner border (top and bottom)
- Cut 9: 1 3/4" x 42" strips, dark green, for the binding
- Cut 4: 5 1/2" squares, gold print, for the border corners

Autumn colors accented by an unexpected touch of purple lend richness to **"Autumn Pines"** *(82 1/2" x 94 1/2"). Jean Wells and quilting friend Ursula Searles planned the quilt. The pieced tree border was inspired by Washington quiltmaker Kathy Sanders. Photo by Ross Chandler*

PIECING

For the 42 Log Cabin blocks:

• Place a red A and a light B, right sides together, and stitch them. As you near the end of the seam, pair another red A and light B and feed them into the machine as you finish the first pair, chain sewing them. Chain sew all of the red A's and light B's this way.

• Clip the threads between the sewn pairs, and press the seam allowances toward B.

• Place an AB unit on top of a light C, right sides together, and stitch. Chain sew all of the light C's to AB units this way.

• Clip threads and press the seam allowances toward C.

• Place an ABC unit on top of a dark D, right sides together, and sew them together, as shown. Chain sew all of the dark D's to the pieced units this way.

• Clip threads and press the seam allowances toward D.

• Place an ABCD unit on a dark E, right sides together, and sew them, as shown. Chain sew all of the dark E's to the pieced units this way. You have created one round. The colors are set with lights on two sides and darks on two sides.

This will alert you to which log to pick up next.

• Continue chain sewing logs to the units in alphabetical order to complete the Log Cabin blocks.

• Arrange the Log Cabin blocks in 7 rows of 6, referring to the quilt photo as needed for placement.

• Stitch the blocks into horizontal rows

(Continued on page 30)

23

Appliqué Tips for "Perfect" Points and More!

Master the skills for flawless stitching.

Quilt artist and teacher Patricia B. Campbell has been making quilts for nearly two decades and is well known for her prizewinning Jacobean appliqué quilts. Soon after learning to quilt, Pat discovered that her passion was appliqué. She began to design her own patterns, translating "fantasy floral" motifs from 17th-century crewel embroidery into graceful and colorful fabric appliqués. Pat also developed appliqué methods for achieving the smooth curves, perfect points and symmetrical circles required for these motifs. She teaches these techniques in popular workshops internationally. Pat is known for her use of vibrant color to enhance the impact of her spectacular quilts. She currently designs a line of fabric for Benartex and Mettler Thread Company offers a Pat Cambell signature collection of machine-weight embroidery threads. Pat also markets a line of her Jacobean appliqué patterns and writes books. Her book titles include *Jacobean Appliqué, Book I* (AQS), *Theorem Appliqué: Abundant Harvest* (Chitra Publications), *Red Hot Chili Peppers* (Texas Stars), *Jacobean Appliqué, Book II* (AQS), *Theorem Appliqué: Summer Splendor* (Chitra Publications) and *Jacobean Rhapsodies* (C&T Publishing). Pat resides in Dallas, Texas, and conducts an annual appliqué retreat in San Antonio with several other appliqué experts. She shares her secrets for appliqué success with tricky shapes like leaves and berries here.

Contact information:
Patricia B. Campbell, 9794 Forest Lane PMB+900, Dallas, TX 75343
Website: Patcampbell.com

Tricky shapes like the leaves and grapes in quilts like "Vitis Vinifera" require appliqué skills that allow you to achieve perfect points and perfectly round circles. The most important secret for making perfect points and round circles is to use a 1/8" turn-under allowance on fabric pieces. With less fabric to turn under, there is less bulk at the points and along the curves.

For practice, choose some fabric scraps with rich colors and textures, and a 14" square of vibrant, dark background fabric. Cut a leaf, a flower and several grapes using the pattern pieces provided on pages 26 and 27. Trace each of the pattern pieces onto template material. Cut the templates out and trace them lightly on the right side of the fabric. Add a 1/8" seam allowance when cutting the fabric pieces out. Pin them on the background square in an arrangement that pleases you and then try my appliqué tips to stitch a square to use as a pillow top or other home accent. If you want to include some vines and stems, I suggest preparing bias strips for appliqué by using bias press bars. Or, if you'd like to try a full-size project like Vitis Vinifera, refer to the materials list on page 26.

Perfect Points

• Start stitching along the side or edge of a motif and stitch toward the point. Never start at the point.

• Just before reaching a point, take a second stitch directly on the last stitch made to secure it.

• Now pull the thread out of the way and hold your thumb over the point. Park your needle by inserting it into the background fabric out of the way and remove your thimble. This allows you to maneuver your middle finger to stabilize the heavy duty "quilter's pin" which you are now going to pick up. (This may seem like a nuisance at first, but give it a chance. Many of my students initially doubt the value of this procedure but soon adopt it into their appliqué routine for keeps!)
NOTE: *A quilter's pin is big—1 3/4"long, with a white head.*

• Use the pin to sweep the allowance from right to left, turning it under. Then with a cupping motion sweep from left to right, turning under the allowance on the other side of the point. Pick up the needle and thread again and take a single stitch in the very point. Continue needle-turning the allowance while stitching down the other side of the appliqué motif. It is not necessary to turn under the allowance where one motif will be overlapped by another.

Smooth circles

• Fabric seems to have a mind of its own. It moves no matter how many pins we use to keep it in place. This can result in a bumpy finish when completing a curve. Therefore, I recommend that you don't mark the shape on the background fabric. This way you don't have to worry about covering the marks when the design piece moves during appliqué. Instead, you can work with the fabric to achieve a smooth finish. If you're not comfortable without background

*"**Vitis Vinifera**" (78" x 89") is the title of this quilt and the botanical name for grapevine. The design represents the vineyard of King James I, with tulips. Study the close-up of the leaf and grape motif in this award-winning beauty! Pat's "perfect" points and perfectly round circles are readily observed in this photo. Practice making your own "perfect" points using Pat's tips and the pattern pieces provided.*

markings, use an "X" to indicate placement for small pieces or mark the shape at least 1/4" inside the edges. This way the markings will not show when the design piece moves.

• While I usually suggest a large sweep with a quilter's pin to turn under the allowance on most appliqué pieces, I recommend just the opposite for circles, ovals and curves. When stitching these, turn under just enough allowance for the next stitch. Using this method works like a charm. Years of practice and often redoing "squared" circles have taught

me to take my time and avoid frustration. I had to redo 120 berries on my "Elizabethan Woods" quilt because the red fabric bled when I washed the quilt. I timed my work and found that when I used the stitch-turn-stitch method, each berry took 10 minutes to complete. When I used the large-sweep method, it still took 10 minutes but I fussed, poked and straightened every one.

• If you can see that a curve is not smooth, try stitching it again. Remove the first four or five stitches. This allows you to re-shape the curve with your needle. Then re-

stitch the area, stitching over two or three of the original stitches to secure them.

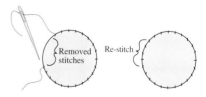

On cutting away layers

I have never cut away the background layers in appliqué because I don't like the look. When I began quiltmaking, my instructors told me cutting away layers would make the design piece stand out by allowing the batting to puff up into the cut-away space. They also said it would make hand quilting easier. However, it seems to me that the opposite happens. The design piece actually sinks! Also, I want my appliqué to "shine" so I do not quilt very much in the design areas, making the layers less of a consideration. I also worry about reducing the stability of the background fabric by cutting it away. Stress on the background fabric from pulling, hanging and handling could cause the design pieces to pull away from it. But perhaps we shouldn't concern ourselves with what our work will look like 100 years from now… or should we? _____QW

Materials List for "Vitis Vinifera" *Yardage is estimated for 44" fabric.*
• 5 1/2 yards background fabric, (I recommend using 100% cotton.)
• Assorted fat quarters and half-yard pieces of fabrics for the appliqués
• 6 1/2 yards fabric for the backing and binding (I suggest using a floral print.)
• Template material
• Assorted cotton machine embroidery thread for appliqué
• Small appliqué pins
• Large "quilter's" pin

Full-Size Leaf and Grape
Appliqué Template Patterns
for "Vitis Vinifera".

Full-Size Tulip Appliqué Template Pattern
for "Vitis Vinifera"
Directions begin on page 24.

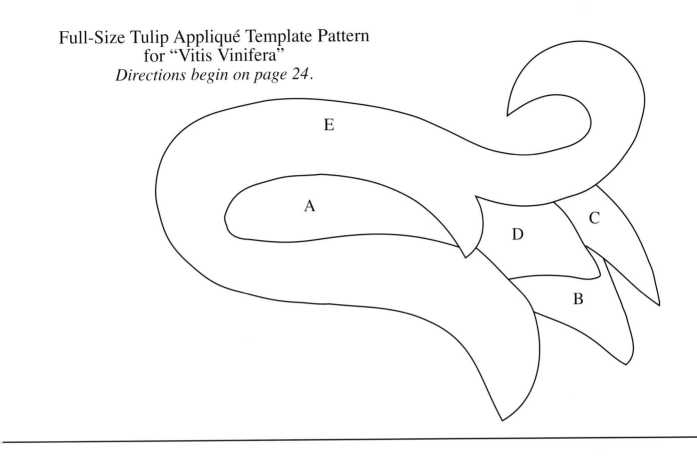

Stencil pattern for
Folkloric Christmas

Directions begin on page 6.

Full-size Leaf and Berry
Stencil Pattern

**Stencil patterns for
Folkloric Christmas**
Directions begin on page 6.

**Full-size Berry Border
stencil pattern**

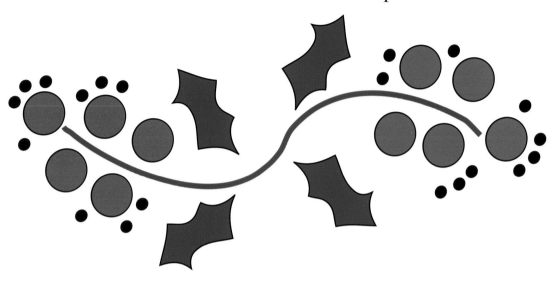

**Full-size
Corner Stencil Pattern**

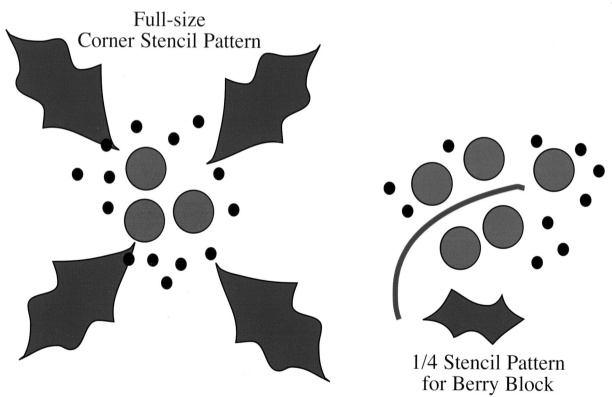

**1/4 Stencil Pattern
for Berry Block**

String-Pieced Star

(continued from page 19)

seam allowance on all sides of the template before cutting it out.

• Make template B in the same manner, marking dots 2" from the indicated star points and drawing lines as shown in the diagram. Use a ruler to draw straight lines from the dots, creating a right angle. Trace the two edges of the star indicated in the diagram in order to complete template B. Remove the star. Add a 1/4" seam allowance on all sides before cutting out the template.

Cutting and piecing background fabric:

• Use the templates to cut setting pieces from the background fabric. You'll need 2 setting pieces made using template A and 4 corner pieces made using template B. Notice that template B needs to be reversed to cut two of the pieces.

• Sew the two setting pieces from template A to opposite sides of the star, pivoting at the angles. Then sew the four pieces from template B to the star, pivoting at the angles.

• Press. Trim to even the edges and square the corners, making sure that the same amount of fabric extends beyond all star points.

Adding borders:

• String piece fabric strips on the 2" by 30" lengths of foundation paper, pressing and trimming, as before. Center and stitch pieced border strips to the long sides of the quilt. Trim the strips even with the edges of the quilt. Center and stitch pieced border strips to the remaining sides of the quilt, trimming, as before.

• Measure the quilt and trim two of the 3" x 33" background fabric strips to this measurement. Stitch them to the long sides of the quilt.

• Measure the quilt, including the borders. Trim the remaining 3" x 33" background fabric strips to this measurement. Sew them to the remaining sides of the quilt.

• Gently remove the paper from the back of the string-pieced sections.

• Finish as described in the *General Directions* using the 2 1/2" x 44" strips for the binding.

_QW

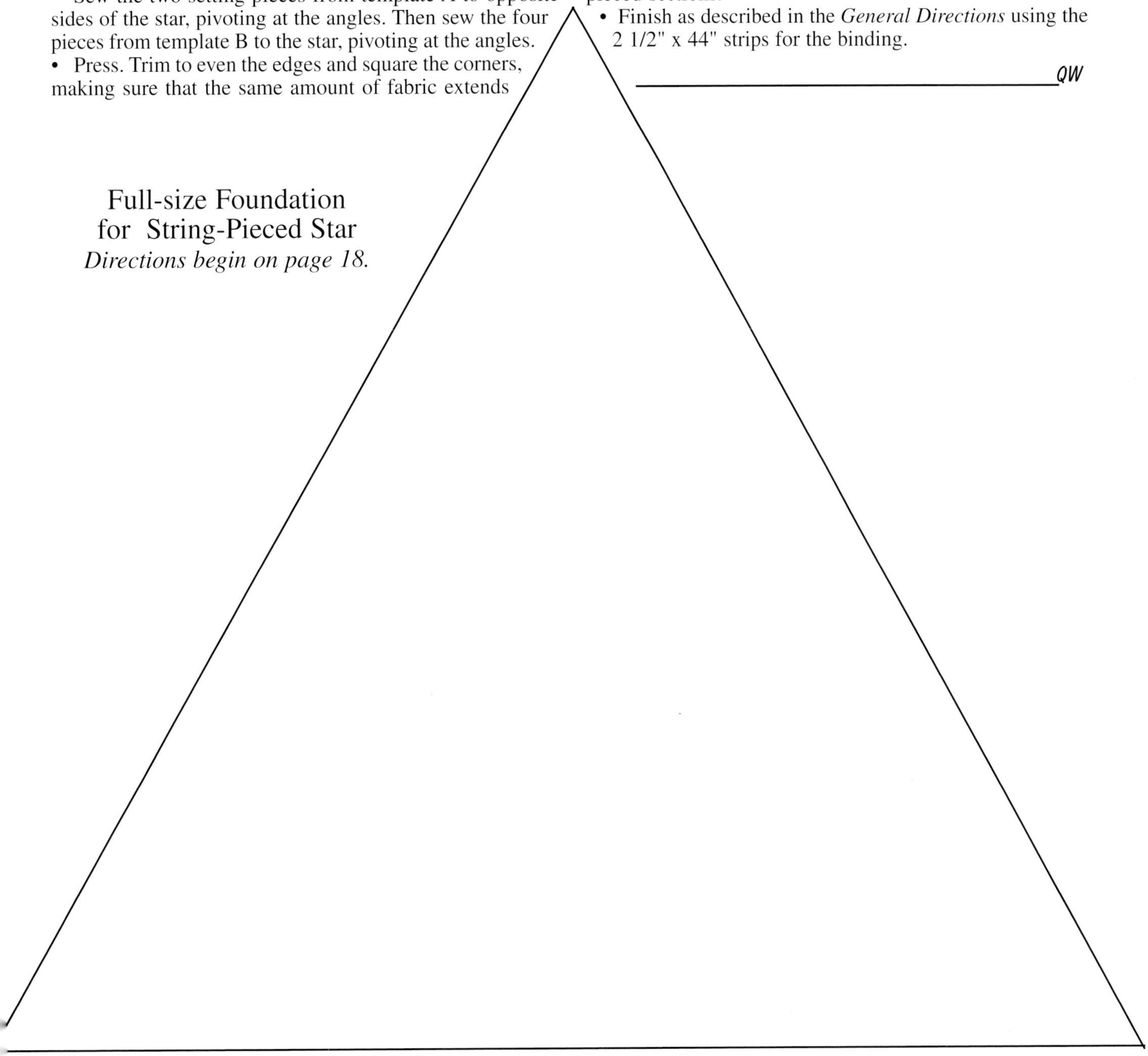

Full-size Foundation for String-Pieced Star

Directions begin on page 18.

Autumn Pines

(continued from page 23)

For the Inner border:

• Join the 2 3/4" x 42" red strips to make one long pieced border strip. From it, cut two strips 79 1/4" long for the long sides of the quilt.

• Join the 3 1/8" x 42" red strips to make one long pieced border strip. From it, cut two strips 72 1/2" long for the short sides of the quilt.

• Stitch the 2 3/4" x 79 1/4" red border strips to the long sides of the quilt, working from the wrong side of the quilt to be sure that seams are stitched down as pressed. Press seam allowances toward the borders.

• Stitch the remaining red border strips to the short sides of the quilt. Press seam allowances as before.

For Row 1 of the Tree border:

• Fold the 2 1/2" gold print squares (B's and D's) in half diagonally and press them to create sewing lines. Open them up.

• Place a 2 1/2" gold print square (B) on one end of a 2 1/2" x 4 1/2" dark green rectangle (A), right sides together. Sew on the pressed line, as shown.

• Trim away the excess fabric, leaving a 1/4" seam allowance. Open the triangle and press the seam allowance toward B.

• In the same manner, sew a 2 1/2" gold print square (B) to the other end of the unit, trimming and pressing as before, to make a double half-square triangle unit. Make 52.

• Lay out 14 double half-square trian-gle units, alternating them with thirteen 2 1/2" gold print squares (G). Join them and sew a 1 1/2" x 2 1/2" gold print rectangle (I) to each end to make a long Row 1. Make 2.

• In the same manner, make 2 short Row 1's using 12 double half-square triangle units, eleven 2 1/2" gold print squares (G) and two 1 1/2" x 2 1/2" gold print rectangles (I).

For Row 2 of the Tree border:

• In the same manner, construct 52 double half-square triangles that are wider than those in Row 1, using the 2 1/2" x 6 1/2" dark green rectangles (C) and the 2 1/2" gold print squares (D).

• Lay out 14 of these units and join them to make a long Row 2. Make 2.

• In the same manner, make two short Row 2's using 12 of the units.

For Row 3 of the Tree border:

• Lay out fourteen 1 1/4" x 1 1/2" brown rectangles (F), alternating them with thirteen 1 1/2" x 5 3/4" gold print rectangles (E). Join them and sew a 1 1/2" x 3 1/8" gold print rectangle (H) to each end to make a long Row 3. Make 2.

• In the same manner, make 2 short Row 3's using twelve 1 1/4" x 1 1/2" brown rectangles (F), eleven 1 1/2" x 5 3/4" gold print rectangles (E) and two 1 1/2" x 3 1/8" gold print rectangles (H).

ASSEMBLY

• Make a long Tree border by joining a long Row 1, 2 and 3, referring to the quilt photo for placement, as necessary. Make 2. In the same manner, make two short Tree borders.

• Sew the long Tree Borders to the long sides of the quilt.

• Sew a 5 1/2" gold print square to each end of the short Tree borders.

• Sew these to the remaining sides of the quilt.

• Finish the quilt by basting and quilting as desired. Join the 1 3/4" dark green strips to make one long pieced binding strip. From it, cut two 94 1/2"-long strips and two 83"-long strips. Press one long edge of each strip under 1/4".

• Place a long binding strip on one long side of the quilt, right sides together and aligning the unpressed edge of the binding with the edge of the quilt top. Sew the binding to the quilt. Trim off the excess batting and back-ing.

• Fold the binding to the back of the quilt and slipstitch it in place, covering the seamline.

• Repeat to stitch binding strips to the remaining long side of the quilt and then the top and bottom. At the corners, fold under the raw edges of the top and bottom bindings even with the side bindings and hand sew them.

QW

California Rail

(continued from page 21)

• Stitch the blocks into rows. Join the rows.

• Measure the length of the quilt. Cut two lengthwise 1 1/2"-wide red print strips to this measurement. Stitch them to the long sides of the quilt.

• Measure the width of the quilt, including the borders. Cut two 1 1/2"-wide red print strips to this measure-ment. Sew them to the remaining sides of the quilt.

• From the reserved pieced strips, cut 2" slices for the border units.

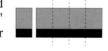

• Measure the length of the quilt. Stitch enough border units together, short end to short end, to create two pieced border strips equal to this mea-surement.

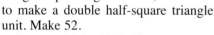

• Stitch them to the sides of the quilt.

• Measure the width of the quilt, including the borders. Stitch enough border units together, short end to short end, to create two pieced border strips equal to this measurement. Stitch them to the remaining sides to complete the quilt top.

• Finish as described in the *General Directions*, using the 2 1/2" x 44" black strips for the binding.

QW

General Directions

Read through directions in the teacher's workshop before cutting fabric for any of the projects. Yardage requirements are based on 44"-wide fabric. Pattern directions are given in step-by-step order.

FABRICS

We suggest using 100% cotton. Wash fabric in warm water with mild detergent and no fabric softener. Wash darks separately and check for bleeding during the rinse cycle. If the color needs to be set, mix equal parts of white vinegar and table salt with water and soak the fabric in it. Dry fabric on a warm-to-hot setting to shrink it. Press with a hot dry iron to remove any wrinkles.

ROTARY CUTTING

Begin by folding the fabric in half, selvage to selvage. Make sure the selvages are even and the folded edge is smooth. Fold the fabric in half again, bringing the fold and the selvages together, again making sure everything is smooth and flat.

Position the folded fabric on a cutting mat so that the fabric extends to the right for right-handed people, or to the left for left-handed people. (Mats with grid lines are recommended because the lines serve as guides to help ensure that cut strips will be straight.)

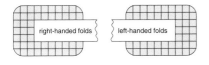

Lay the fabric so that the folded edge is along one of the horizontal lines on the mat. Place the ruler on one of the vertical lines, just over the uneven edges of the fabric. The ruler must be absolutely perpendicular to the folded edge. Trim the uneven edges with a rotary cutter. Hold the rotary cutter at a 45° angle to the mat. Make a clean cut through the fabric, beginning in front of the folds and cutting through to the opposite edge with one clean (not short and choppy) stroke. Always cut away from yourself—never toward yourself!

Move the ruler to the proper width for cutting the first strip and continue cutting until you have the required number of strips. To keep the cut edges even, always move the ruler, not the fabric. Open up one fabric strip and check the spots where there were folds. If the fabric was not evenly lined up or the ruler was incorrectly positioned, there will be a bend at each of the

folds in the fabric.

When cutting many strips, check after every four or five strips to make sure the strips are straight. Leave the strips folded in fourths until you are ready to use them.

APPLIQUÉ

To make templates place a sheet of firm, clear plastic over the patterns and trace the cutting line for each one. Templates for appliqué do not include a seam allowance.

Test marking tools for removability before using them. Sharpen pencils often. Place a piece of fine sandpaper beneath the fabric to prevent slipping, if desired.

Trace the templates on the right side of the fabric. Add a 1/8" seam allowance when cutting the pieces out. Handle bias edges carefully to avoid stretching. Mark the position of the pieces on the background as directed in the workshop.

PIECING

When machine piecing, sew 12 stitches per inch, exactly 1/4" from the edge of the fabric. If necessary, mark the throat plate with a piece of tape 1/4" away from the point where the needle pierces the fabric. Backstitching is not necessary. Start and stop stitching at the cut edges except for set-in pieces. For set-ins, start and stop 1/4" from the edges of the piece and backstitch.

FOUNDATION PIECING

Foundation piecing is a method for making blocks with a high degree of accuracy. For each foundation, trace all of the lines and numbers onto paper, muslin or lightweight non-fusible interfacing, as indicated in the pattern. You will need one foundation for each block. The solid line is the stitching line and the broken line is the cutting line. The fabric pieces you select do not have to be cut precisely. Be generous when cutting fabric pieces as excess fabric will be trimmed away after sewing. Your goal is to cut a piece that covers the numbered area and extends into surrounding areas after seams are stitched. Generally, fabric pieces should be large enough to extend 1/2" beyond the seamline on all sides before stitching.

You'll notice that, with certain designs, the foundation pattern is the reverse of the finished block. That's because, when stitching the block, fabric pieces are placed on the unmarked side of the foundation and stitched on the marked side. Center the first piece, right side up, over position 1 on the unmarked side of the foundation. Hold the foundation up to a light to make sure that the raw edges of the fabric extend at least 1/2" beyond the seamline on all sides. Hold this first piece in place with a small dab of glue or a pin. Place the fabric for position 2 on the first piece, right sides together. Turn the foundation over and sew on the line between 1 and 2, extending the

stitching past the beginning and end of the line by a few stitches on both ends. Trim the seam allowance to 1/4". Fold the position 2 piece back, right side up, and press. Continue adding pieces to the foundation in the same manner until all positions are covered and the block is complete.

If you are using a muslin or interfacing foundation, it will become a permanent part of the quilt. If you are using paper, it will be removed. However, do not remove the paper until directed to do so in the pattern, to avoid disturbing the stitches. The pieces will be perforated from the stitching and can be gently pulled free. Use tweezers to carefully remove pieces of the paper, if necessary.

PRESSING

Press with a dry iron. Press seam allowances toward the darker of the two pieces unless directed to do otherwise in the pattern. In that case, trim away 1/16" from the darker seam allowance to prevent it from showing through, if necessary. Press all blocks, sashings and borders before assembling the quilt top. Press appliqué blocks from the wrong side, on a towel to prevent a flat, shiny look.

MARKING QUILTING LINES

Mark before basting the quilt together with the batting and backing. Chalk pencils show well on dark fabrics; otherwise use a very hard (#3 or #4) pencil or other marker for this purpose. Test your marker first. Transfer paper designs by placing fabric over the design and tracing. A light box may be necessary for darker fabrics. Precut plastic stencils that fit the area you wish to quilt may be placed on top of the quilt and traced. Use a ruler to mark straight, even grids.

Outline quilting does not require marking. Simply eyeball 1/4" from the seam or stitch "in the ditch" next to the seam or the neighboring patch. To prevent uneven stitching, try to avoid quilting through seam allowances wherever possible.

Masking tape can also be used to mark straight lines. Temporary quilting stencils can be made from clear adhesive-backed paper or freezer paper and reused many times. To avoid residue, do not leave tape or adhesive-backed paper on your quilt overnight.

BASTING

Cut the batting and backing at least 2" larger on all sides than the quilt top. Tape the backing, wrong side up, on a flat surface to anchor it. Smooth the batting on top, followed by the quilt top, right side up. Baste the three layers together to form a quilt sandwich. Begin at the center and baste horizontally, then vertically. Add more lines of basting approximately every 6" until the entire top is secured.

QUILTING

Quilting is done with a short, strong needle called a "between." The lower the number (size) of the needle, the larger it is. Begin with an 8 to 9 and progress to a 10 to 12. Use a thimble on the middle finger of the hand that pushes the needle. When you let your hand hang down at your side and move it slightly, the thimble should remain on the finger but not feel constricting. Rather than a specific number of stitches per inch, your goal in hand quilting should be to make even, consistent stitches. The method used by most hand quilters to achieve this is known as the rocking stitch. Begin quilting at the center of the quilt and work outward to keep the tension even and the quilting smooth.

Thread the needle by inserting the end of the thread through the eye while the thread is still on the spool. This helps prevent fraying, which makes threading difficult. Cut a 17" length of thread and make a small knot in the end that you cut from the spool. Insert the needle through the quilt top and batting only and bring it up exactly where you will begin. Pull the needle and thread until the knot lies on top of the quilt top at the insertion point. Pop the knot through the fabric to bury it. You may find that using the thumbnail of your non-quilting hand to apply some pressure on the fabric near the knot helps it to pop through more easily.

The Rocking Stitch

Place your underneath hand beneath the layers where you'll begin quilting. Hold the needle gently between your thumb and forefinger. Position the needle about 1/8" from the starting point so that it is perpendicular to the quilt top, placing the thimble at the eye-end of 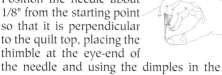 the needle and using the dimples in the thimble to "grip" and balance the needle. Then insert the tip of the needle straight down through all layers, until you can just feel the tip with your underneath hand (usually on the pad of your index or middle finger).

When you feel the tip, release the needle and use the thimble to rock the eye of the needle down so the needle lies parallel to the marked quilting line and the tip of the needle moves up.

At the same time, press down on the layers with the thumb of your quilting hand slightly ahead of the insertion point and press up slightly on the layers with the underneath finger. This will create a "hill" in the fabric layers.

Put pressure on the eye-end of the needle with the thimble to guide the needle tip up through all three layers on the marked line and at the top of the hill.

Keeping pressure on the needle with the thimble, use the thumb of your quilting hand to push the hill and work the needle through the layers far enough so that you can grip it between the thumb and forefinger of the quilting hand.

Remove the thimble from the needle, releasing pressure, and move the thumb and forefinger to the shank of the needle. Use them to pull the needle and thread through.

Tug slightly to secure the stitch and cause it to lie down into the fibers of the quilt top. However, don't pull so tight that the thread gets buried. This creates too much tension on the thread and can give the quilting an undesirable puckered look.

Once you have mastered these steps for making one stitch at a time, you're ready to take three to four stitches on the needle at a time to increase your speed.

Follow the steps previously outlined, except do not push the hill to work the needle through the fabric layers far enough to grip it between the thumb and forefinger of the quilting hand. Instead, leave just the tip exposed at the top of the hill. With the thimble still on the eye-end of the needle, rock the thimble straight up so that the needle is perpendicular to the quilt layers again. Guide the needle tip down through the three layers until you can feel it with the underneath hand, as before.

When you feel the tip, use the thimble to rock the needle down so it again lies parallel to the marked line. At the same time, press down on the layers with the thumb of the quilting hand and up with the underneath finger to make a hill as before.

Use the thimble to put pressure on the eye end of the needle and guide the tip up through all three layers on the marked line at the top of the hill. Leaving the tip exposed, rock the needle down and make a third stitch in the same manner.

After the third stitch, keep pressure on the needle with the thimble and use the thumb of your quilting hand to push the hill, working the needle through the layers far enough to grip it, as before.

When there are about 5" of thread left, you're ready to end off. Make a small knot close to the last hole the needle came through. Do this using your favorite method or by forming the thread into a loop and bringing the needle through it. Use your fingers to keep the knot close to the hole (1/4" or less away) while pulling the thread through.

Insert the needle back into the hole and direct it away from the line of quilting, sliding it through the batting for about 1/2". Bring the needle through to the quilt top and tug the thread to bury the knot in the batting. Remove basting when all the quilting is done.

If you wish to machine quilt, we recommend consulting one of the many excellent books available on the subject.

BINDING

Trim excess batting and backing even to within 1/4" of the quilt top. Cut binding strips with the grain for straight-edge quilts. To make 1/2" finished binding, cut 2 1/2" wide strips. Sew strips together with diagonal seams; trim and press seams open.

Fold the strip in half lengthwise, right side out and press. Position the strip on the right side of the quilt top, aligning the raw edges of the binding with the edge of the quilt top, (not so that all raw edges are even.) Leaving 6" free and beginning a few inches from one corner, stitch the binding to the quilt with a 1/2" seam allowance measuring from the raw edge of the backing. When you reach a corner, stop stitching 1/2" from the edge and backstitch. Clip threads and remove the quilt from the machine. Fold the binding up and away from the quilt, forming a 45° angle as shown. Keeping the angled fold secure, fold the binding back down. This fold should be even with the edge of the quilt top. Begin stitching at the fold through all the layers.

Continue stitching around the quilt in this manner to within 6" of the starting point. To finish, fold both strips back along the edge of the quilt so that the folded edges meet 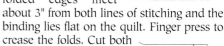 about 3" from both lines of stitching and the binding lies flat on the quilt. Finger press to crease the folds. Cut both strips 1 1/4" from the folds.

Open both strips and place the ends at right angles to each other, right sides together. Fold the bulk of the quilt out of your way. Join the strips with a diagonal seam as shown.

Trim the seam to 1/4" and press it open. Fold the joined strips so that the wrong sides are together again. Place the binding flat against the quilt and finish stitching it to the quilt. Trim the layers as needed so that the binding edge will be filled with batting when you fold the binding to the back of the quilt. Blindstitch the binding to the back, covering the seamline.

FINISHING

Remove visible markings. Sign and date your quilt.